Pippa and Pop

3 Letters and Numbers Workbook

	My letters	My numbers
1 Page 2	Tracing and recognizing letters *a to z*	*1* to *10*
2 Page 8	Tracing words about daily activities	*1* to *20*
3 Page 14	Tracing words about the home	*30, 40*
4 Page 20	Writing words about sport	*10* to *40*
5 Page 26	Writing words about activities	*10* to *60*

	My letters	My numbers
6 Page 32	Tracing words and sentences about food	*10* to *80*
7 Page 38	Tracing sentences about animals	*10* to *80*
8 Page 44	Writing sentences about plants and adjectives	*80* to *100*
9 Page 50	Forming and writing sentences about professions and places	Numbers *1* to *100*

Trace.

Review the alphabet. Then the children identify and trace the letters with colored pencils.

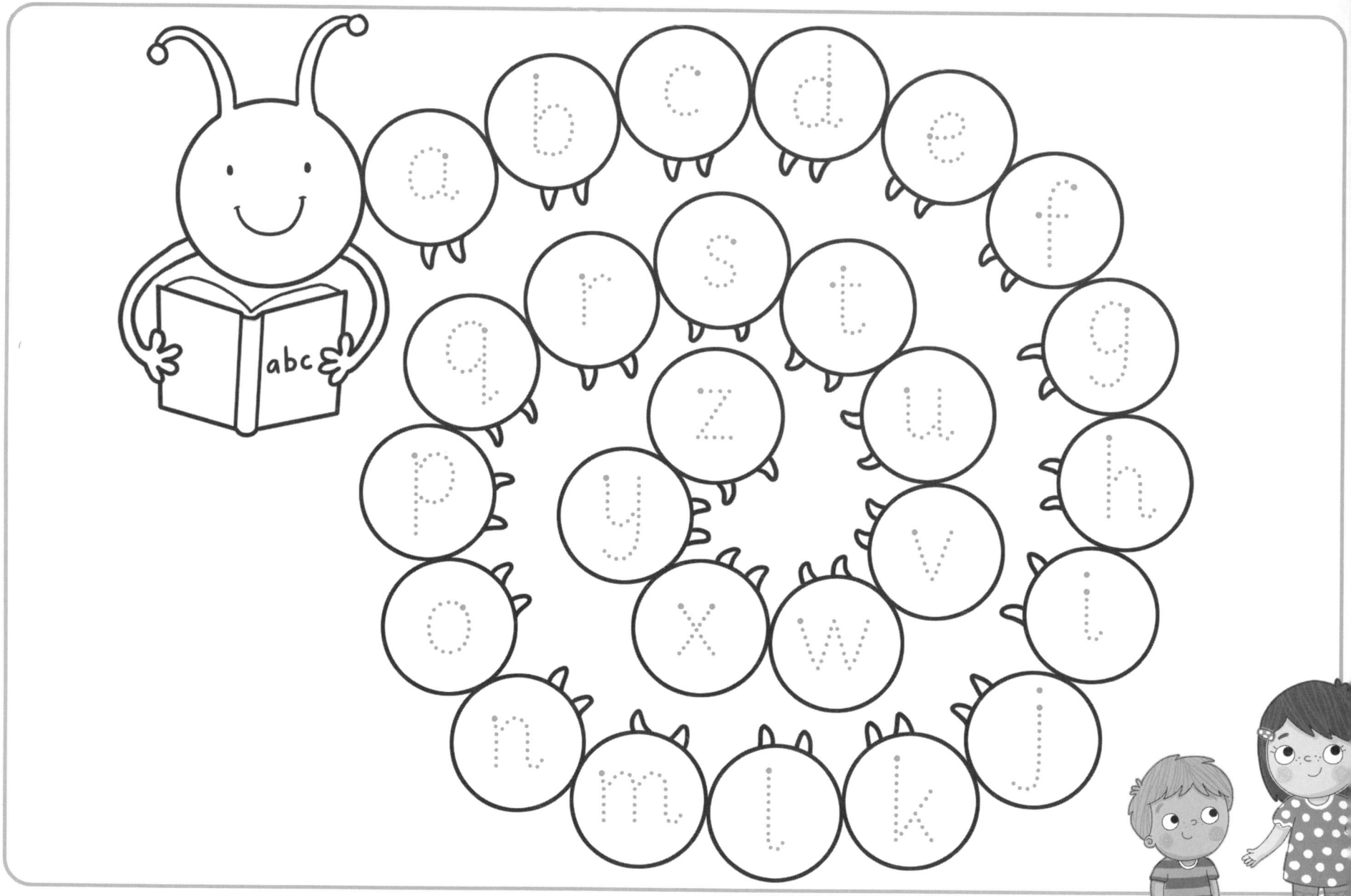

Match. Color.

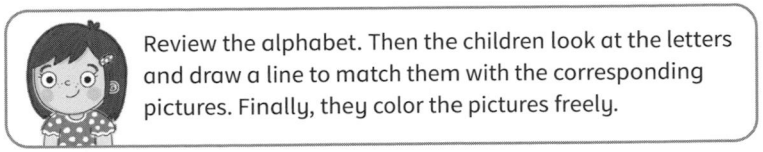

Review the alphabet. Then the children look at the letters and draw a line to match them with the corresponding pictures. Finally, they color the pictures freely.

a c e g j m

Circle. Color.

The children circle the letter each picture starts with. Then they color in the pictures freely.

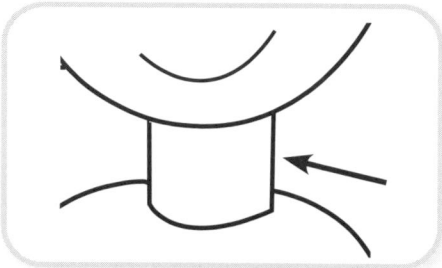

n j f l

d t r q

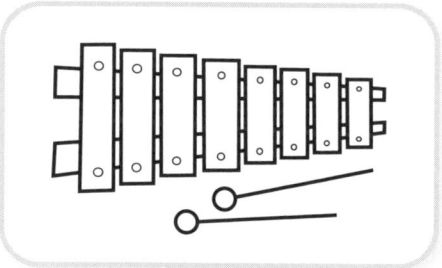

w x v y

b s z k

Count. Circle. Color.

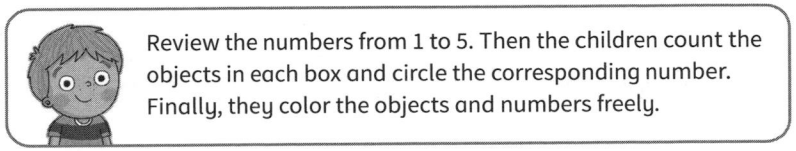

Review the numbers from 1 to 5. Then the children count the objects in each box and circle the corresponding number. Finally, they color the objects and numbers freely.

2 5

4 3

2 1

1 4

4 5

5 3

Trace. Count. Color.

Review the numbers from 1 to 10. Then the children point to the number 9, trace it and count and color nine crayons. Repeat the procedure for the remaining numbers and items.

Write. Color.

Review the numbers from 1 to 10. Then the children look at the first series of numbers and write the missing number. Repeat the procedure for the remaining series. Finally, they color the pictures freely.

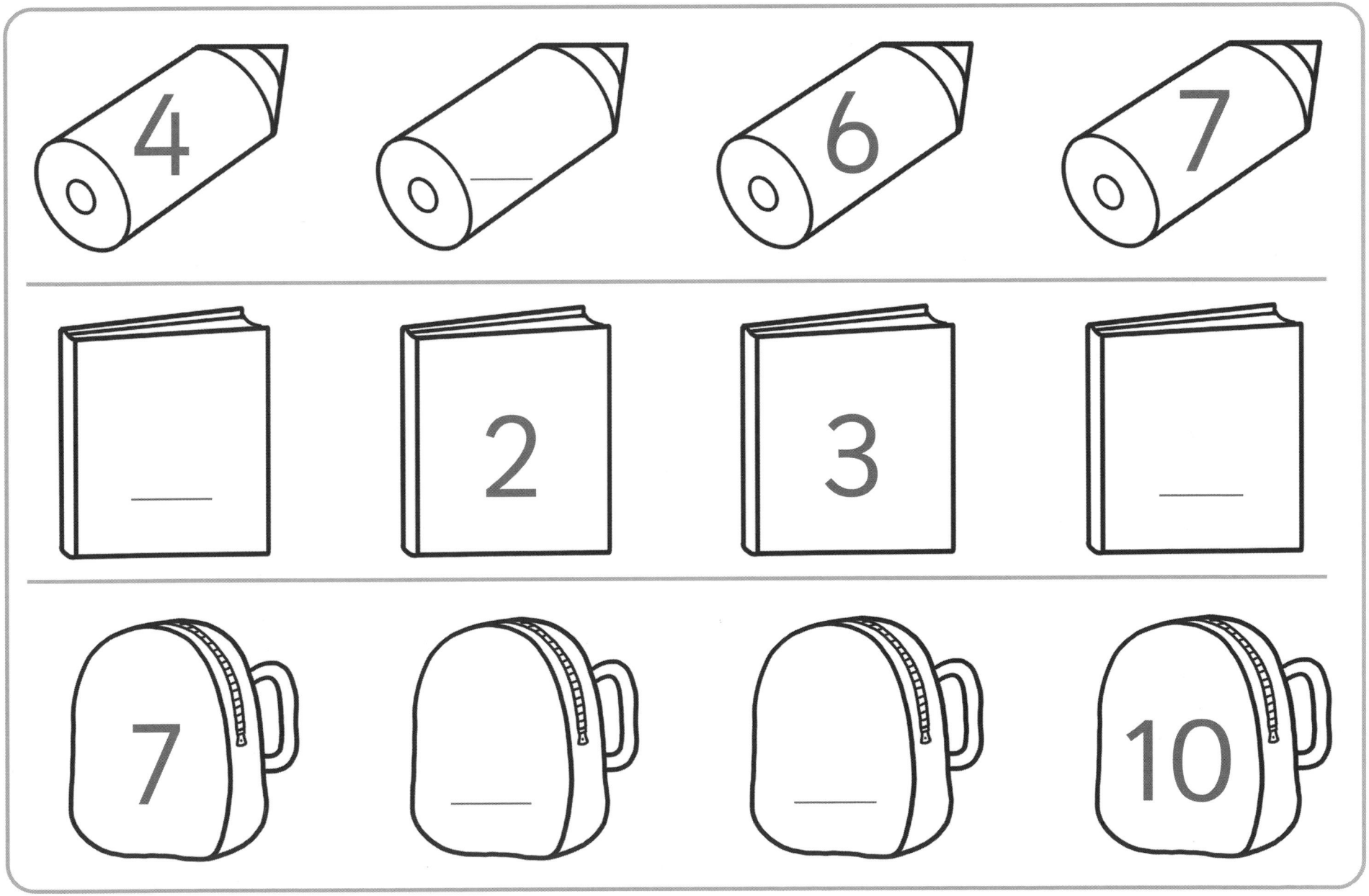

Trace. Color.

The children identify the daily activities.
Then they trace the words with colored pencils.
Finally, the children color the pictures freely.

have breakfast

brush my teeth

wake up

get dressed

Trace. Color.

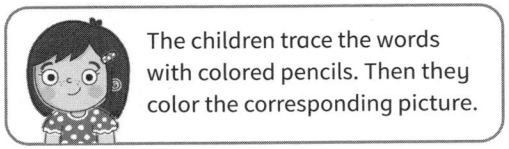

The children trace the words with colored pencils. Then they color the corresponding picture.

I wash my face.

I brush my hair.

I have breakfast.

Trace. Match. Color.

The children trace the words with colored pencils. Then they match the sentences with the corresponding pictures. Finally, the children color the pictures freely.

I wake up every day.

I get dressed every day.

I wash my face every day.

Follow. Draw. Color.

Review the numbers from 1 to 20. Then the children connect the dots. Ask *What is it? A house!* Finally, they color the house freely.

Count. Match. Color.

Review the numbers from 1 to 20. Then the children count the dots on each bed. Next, they draw lines to match the dots on the beds with the corresponding numbers. Finally, the children color the pictures freely.

10 4 14 20

Count. Write.

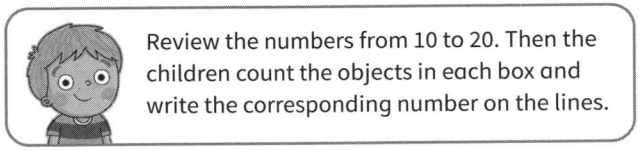

Review the numbers from 10 to 20. Then the children count the objects in each box and write the corresponding number on the lines.

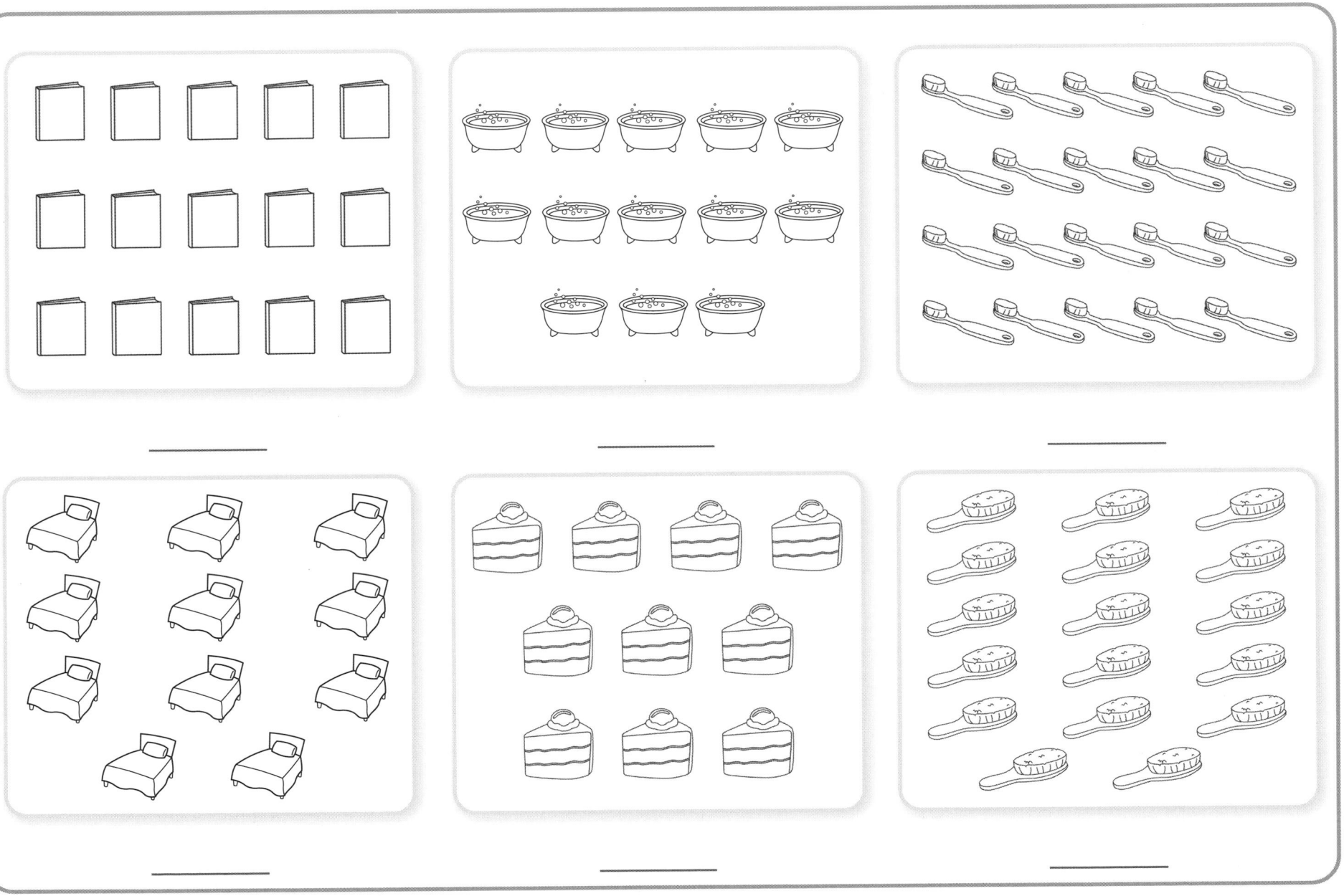

Match. Trace. Color.

The children trace over each path with a red crayon. Then they trace the corresponding words with colored pencils. Finally, the children color the pictures.

bed

toy box

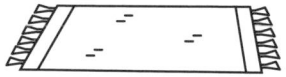

lamp

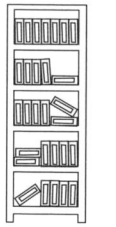

rug

cabinet

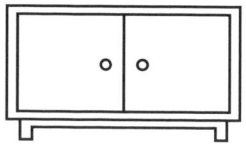

bookcase

Trace. Match. Color.

The children trace the words with colored pencils. Then they draw lines to match the sentences with the corresponding pictures. Finally, the children color the pictures freely.

It's next to the cabinet.

It's on the bed.

It's in the toy box.

Trace. Circle.

The children trace the words with colored pencils. Then they circle the correct pictures.

It's under the rug.

It's on the bookcase.

It's next to the lamp.

Count. Color.

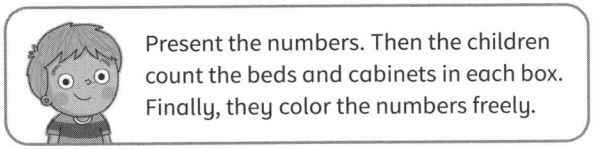

Present the numbers. Then the children count the beds and cabinets in each box. Finally, they color the numbers freely.

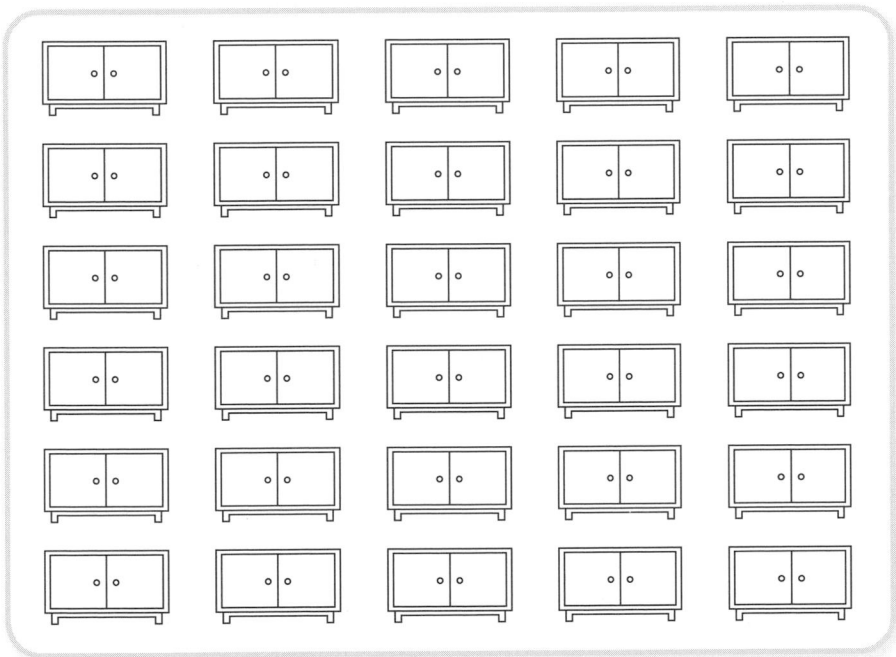

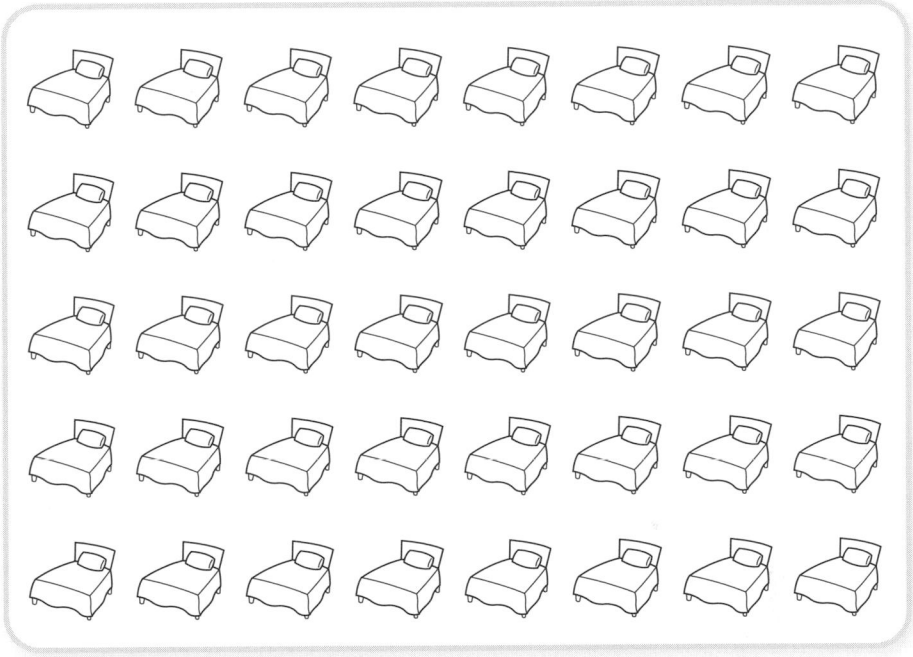

30

40

Count. Circle.

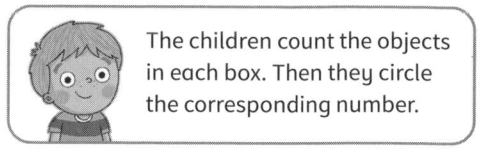

The children count the objects in each box. Then they circle the corresponding number.

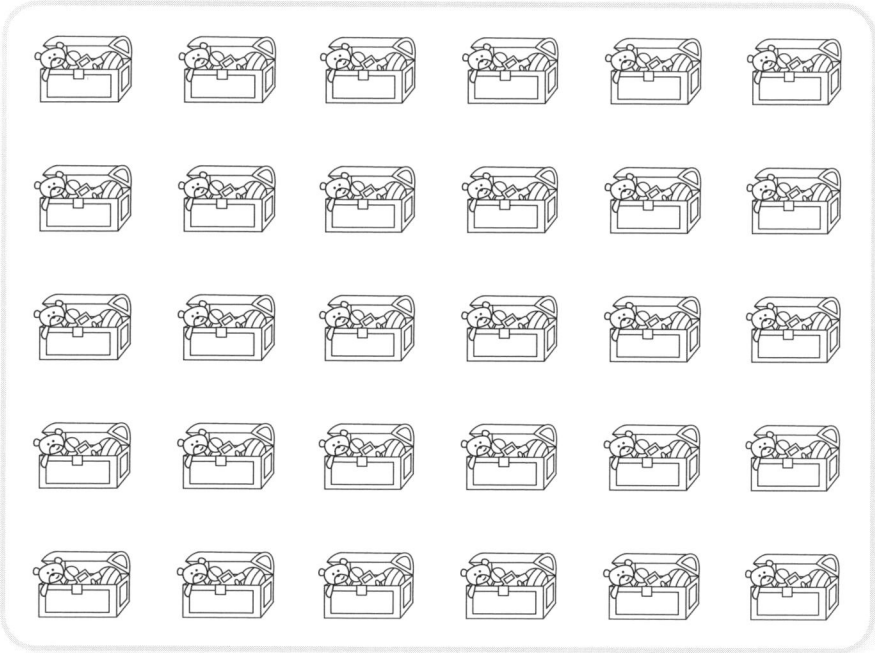

30 40

30 40

Count. Draw.

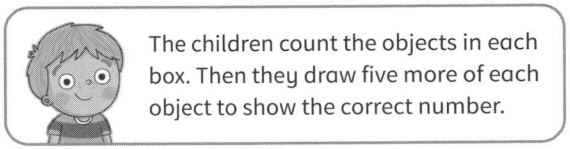
The children count the objects in each box. Then they draw five more of each object to show the correct number.

= 30

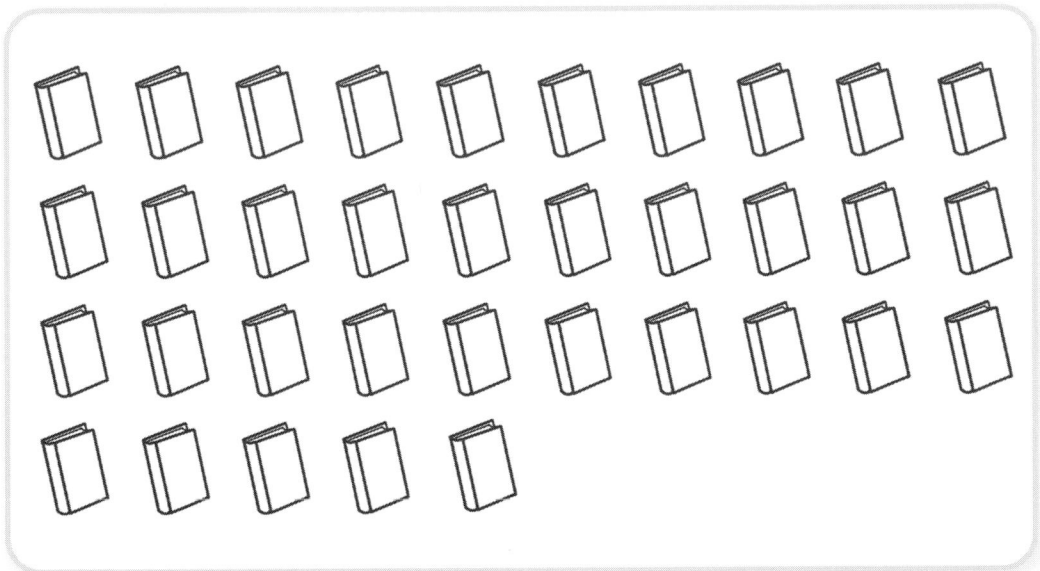

= 40

Write. Color.

The children write the words in the boxes under the correct sport. Then they color the pictures freely.

badminton
field hockey
baseball
soccer
basketball
tennis

Circle. Write.

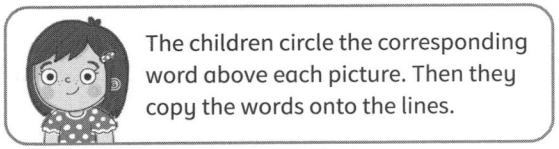

The children circle the corresponding word above each picture. Then they copy the words onto the lines.

badminton basketball

He's playing .

baseball tennis

She's playing .

baseball soccer

They're playing .

Circle. Write.

The children look at the first picture and circle the word that best completes the first sentence. Then they copy the word onto the line. Repeat the procedure for the remaining pictures and sentences.

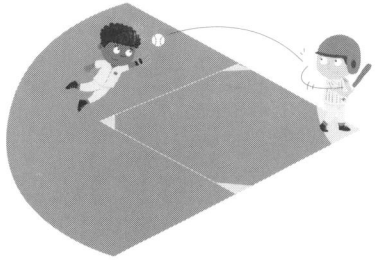

field hockey
baseball

They're playing _____.

basketball
soccer

They're playing _____.

badminton
tennis

They're playing _____.

Count. Match. Color.

The children count the balls in each box and match the boxes with the corresponding numbers. Then they color the numbers freely.

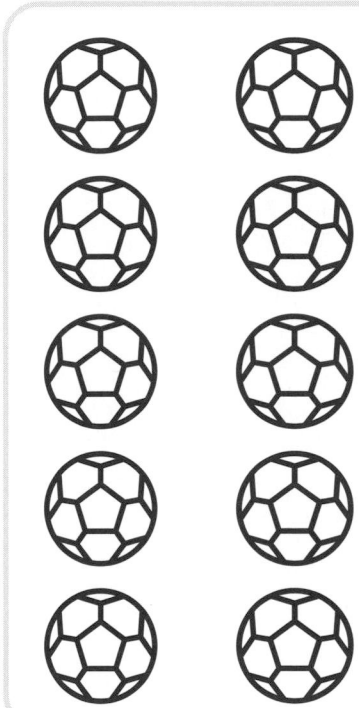

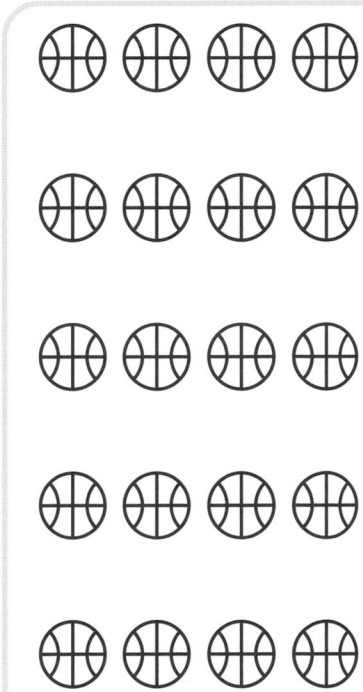

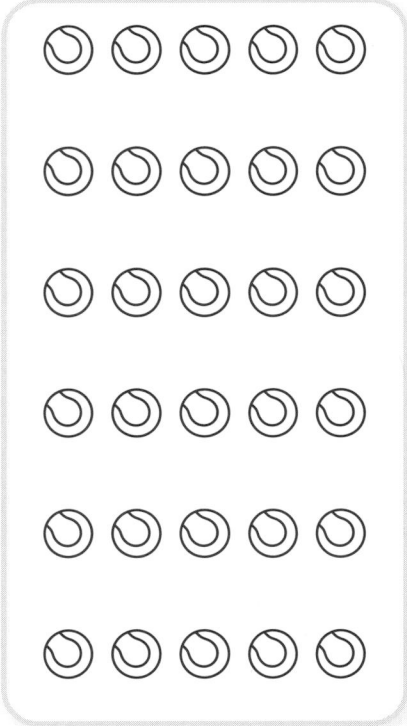

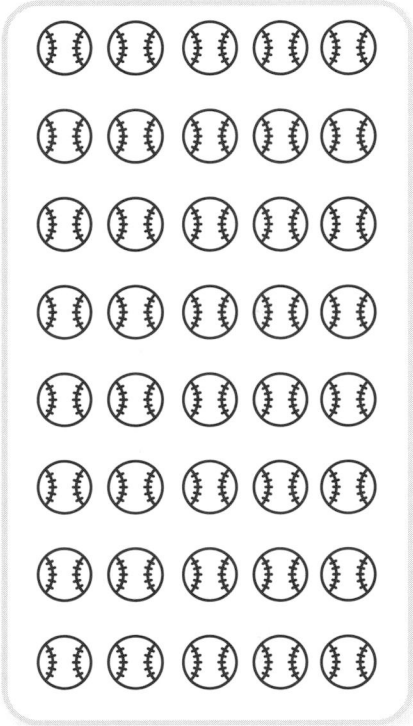

30 40 10 20

Count. Trace.

The children count the objects in each box. Then they trace the corresponding number.

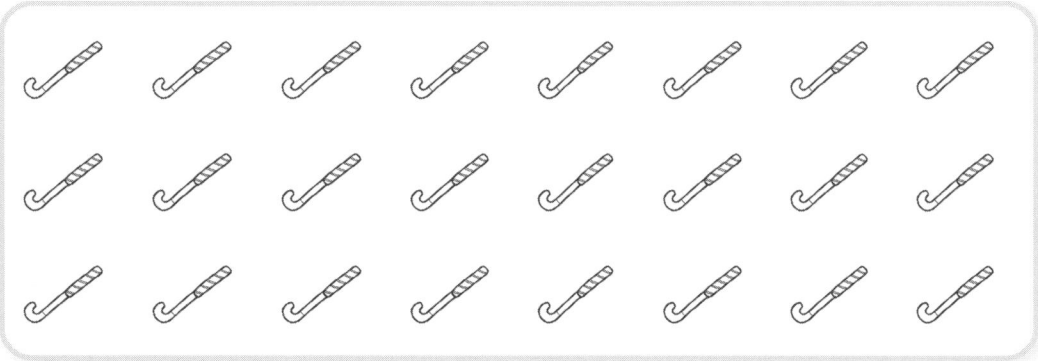

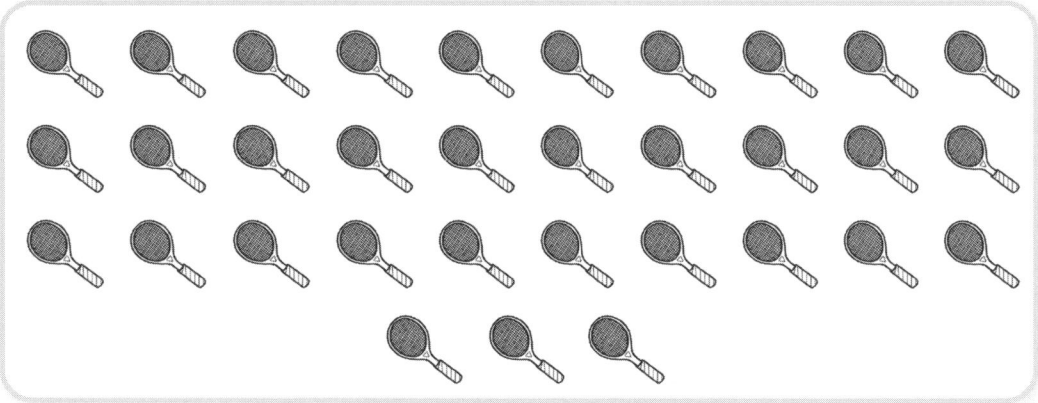

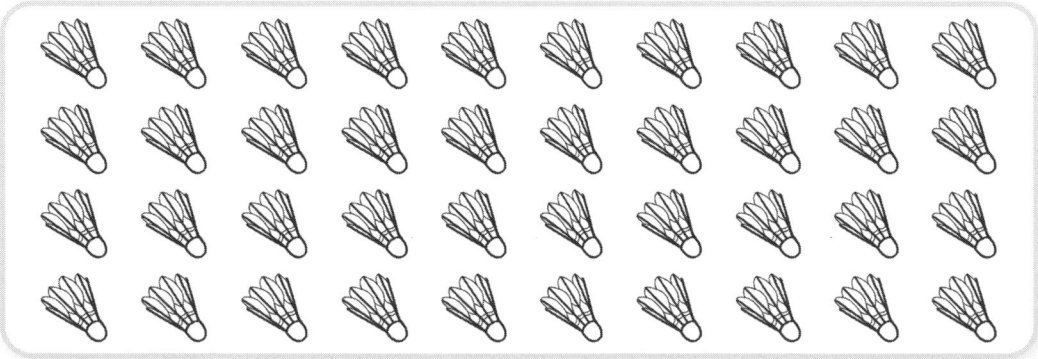

20 24

33 35

29 40

Write. Color.

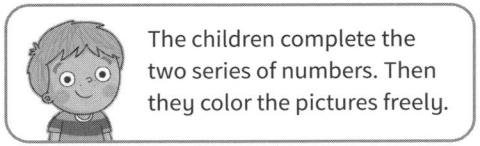

The children complete the two series of numbers. Then they color the pictures freely.

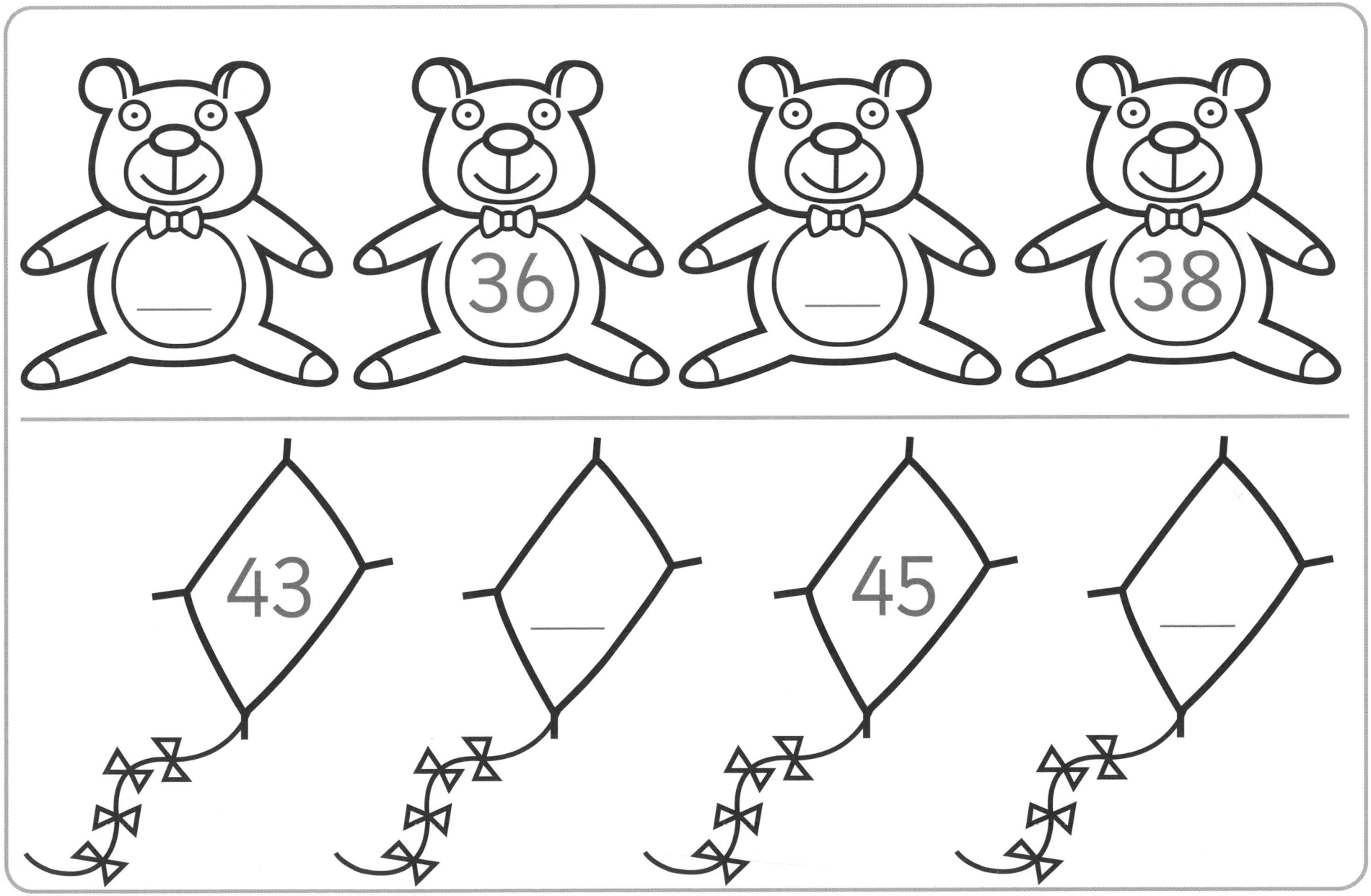

Write. Color.

The children write the correct phrase under the picture. Then they color the pictures freely.

reading books

listening to music

watching TV

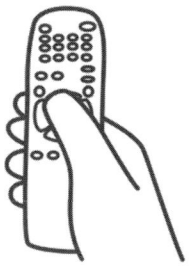

Trace. Write. Color.

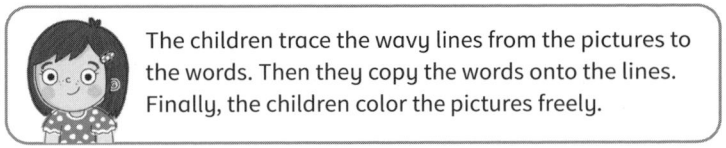
The children trace the wavy lines from the pictures to the words. Then they copy the words onto the lines. Finally, the children color the pictures freely.

drawing

pictures

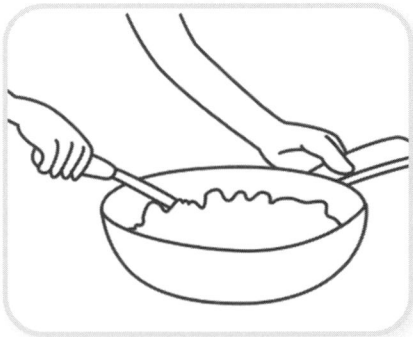

cooking

dinner

playing

video games

Write. Color.

The children copy the words onto the lines to complete each sentence. Then they color the pictures freely.

We like _____.

reading books

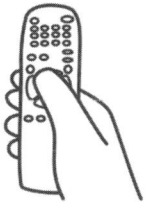

I like _____.

watching TV

I like _____.

drawing pictures

Count. Trace. Color.

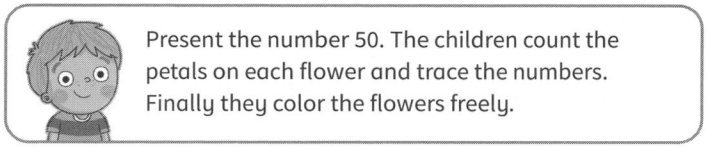

Present the number 50. The children count the petals on each flower and trace the numbers. Finally they color the flowers freely.

10

20

30

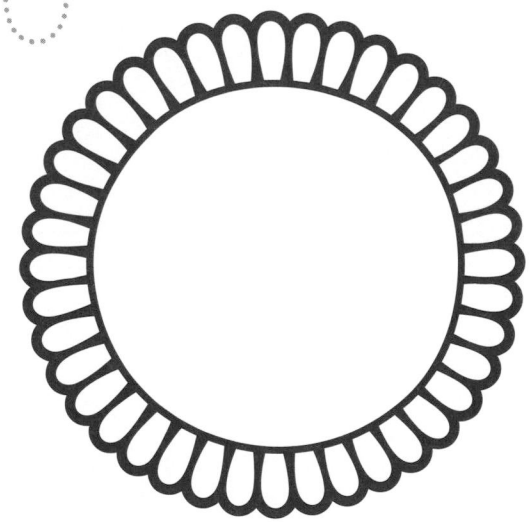

40

50

Count. Color.

Present the number 60. Then the children count the bubbles in the bathtubs in sets of tens. Finally, they color the pictures freely.

60

Count. Circle.

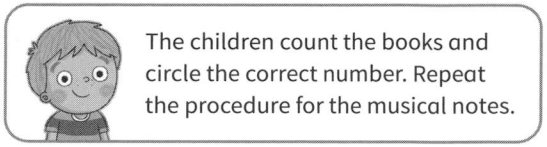

The children count the books and circle the correct number. Repeat the procedure for the musical notes.

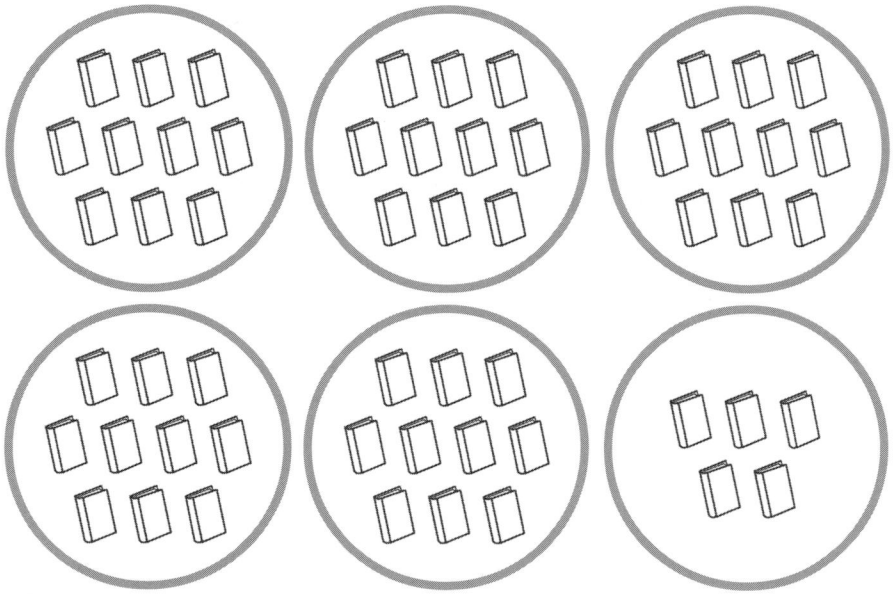

= 55 53 60

= 58 60 57

Unit 6

Trace. ✔ Write a check.

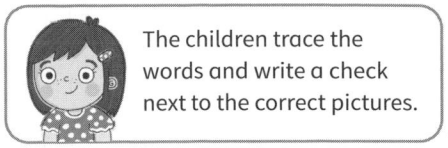

The children trace the words and write a check next to the correct pictures.

chocolate

grapes

pineapple

Trace. Circle.

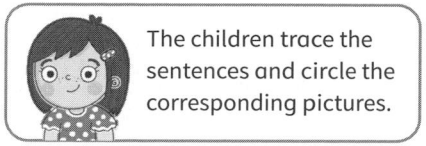

The children trace the sentences and circle the corresponding pictures.

Would you like some sweets?

Would you like some chips?

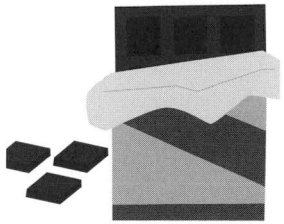

Would you like some cake?

Trace. Match.

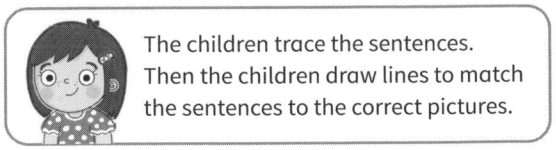
The children trace the sentences.
Then the children draw lines to match the sentences to the correct pictures.

I'd like some cake.

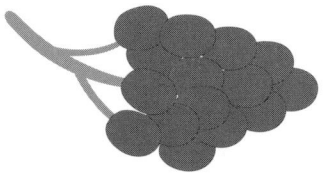

I'd like some chocolate.

I'd like some grapes.

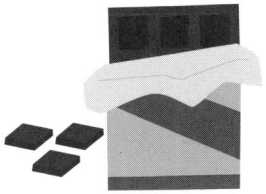

Count. Trace. Color.

The children identify and count the pineapples. Then they trace the number that corresponds to the total number of pineapples. Repeat the same procedure for the remaining food items. Finally, the children color the pictures freely.

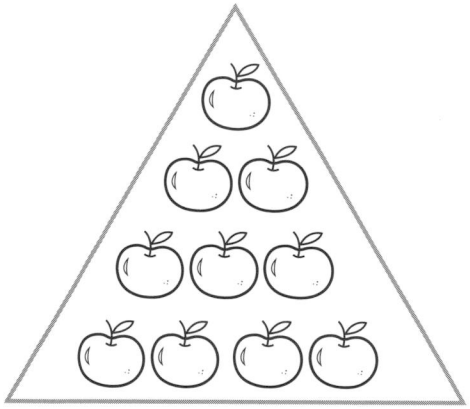

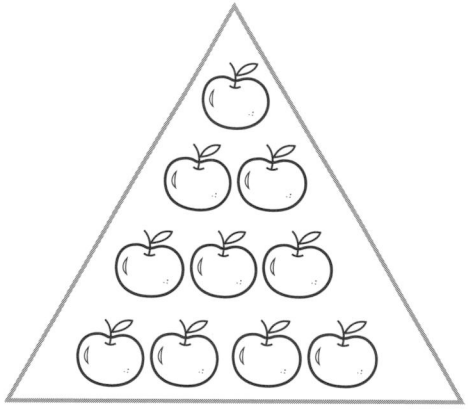

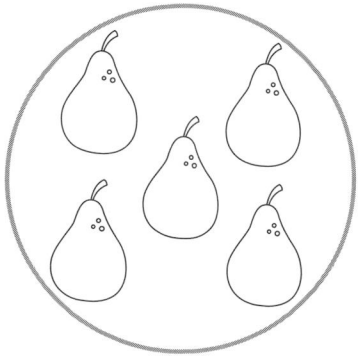

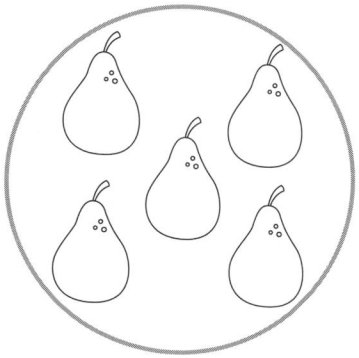

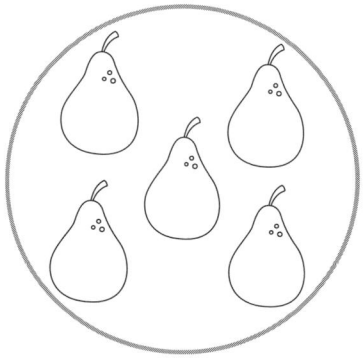

14 18

16 20

15 17

Count. Write. Color.

The children count the food items in each box. Then they write the corresponding number next to each picture. Finally, the children color the pictures freely.

How many?

_____

_____

_____

Write. Color.

Review the numbers from 10 to 80. Then the children look at the picture and write the missing numbers. Finally, they color the picture freely.

10

40

80

Trace. Draw. Color.

The children trace the sentences. Then they draw and color the animals' missing body parts. Finally, the children color the animals freely.

There's a monkey.

There's a tiger.

There's a snake.

Trace. Count. Circle.

The children trace the sentences with colored pencils. Then they circle the correct number of elephants, hippos and crocodiles.

There are two elephants.

There are three hippos.

There are four crocodiles.

Trace. Draw.

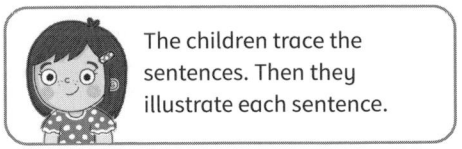

The children trace the sentences. Then they illustrate each sentence.

There's a snake.

There are two elephants.

There are three hippos.

Count. Paint.

Present the number 70. Next, the children count the sheep in tens. Finally, the children paint the number 70. Alternatively, they can color the number with crayons.

Count. Color.

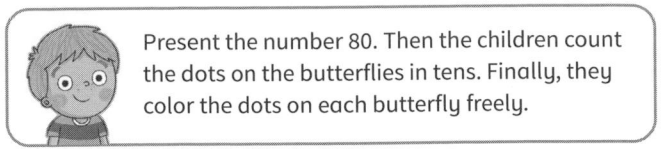
Present the number 80. Then the children count the dots on the butterflies in tens. Finally, they color the dots on each butterfly freely.

Follow. Draw. Color.

Review the numbers from 1 to 80. Then the children connect the dots and form a rabbit. Finally, they color the rabbit freely.

Read. Write. Color.

The children copy the sentences onto the lines. Then they color the pictures freely.

Plants need rain.

Plants

Plants need soil.

Plants need sun.

Read. Circle. Write.

The children read the sentences and circle the correct pictures. Then they copy the sentences onto the lines.

What beautiful flowers!

What ..... !

What an old hat!

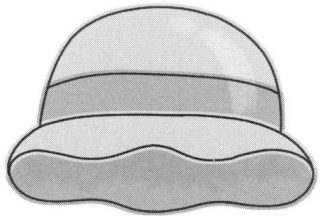

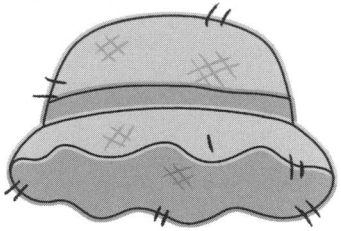

..... !

Read. ✔ Write a check. Write.

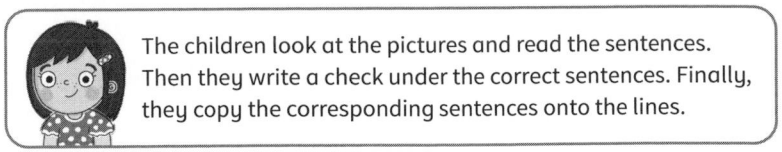

The children look at the pictures and read the sentences. Then they write a check under the correct sentences. Finally, they copy the corresponding sentences onto the lines.

Plants need rain. ☐

Plants need sun. ☐

Plants .

What an ugly garden! ☐

What a beautiful garden! ☐

!

Count. Color.

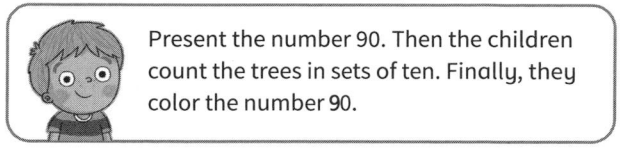

Present the number 90. Then the children count the trees in sets of ten. Finally, they color the number 90.

90

Count. Color.

Present the number 100. The children count the suns in sets of ten. Then they color the number 100 freely.

100

Count. Circle.

Review the numbers from 80 to 100. Then the children count the seeds and circle the corresponding number. Repeat the procedure for the leaves.

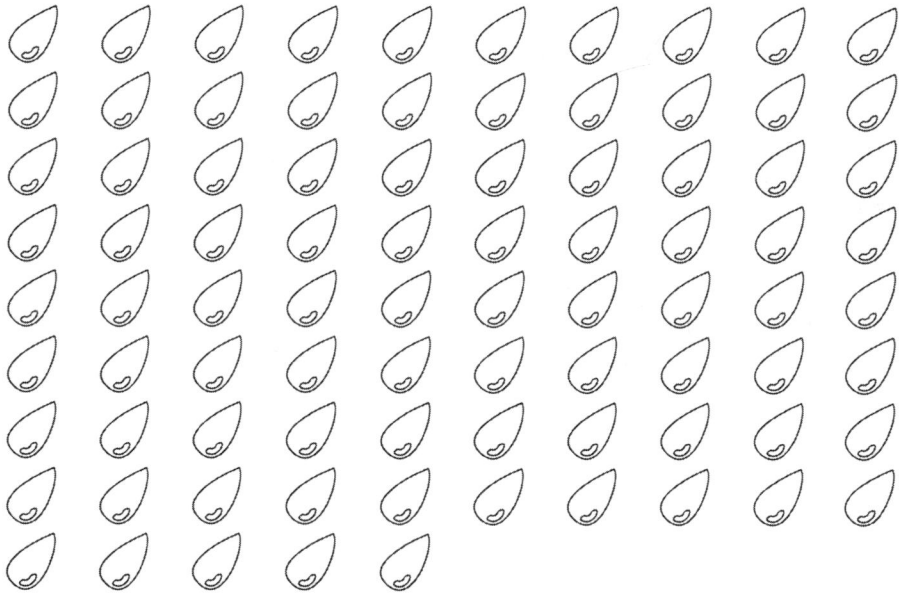

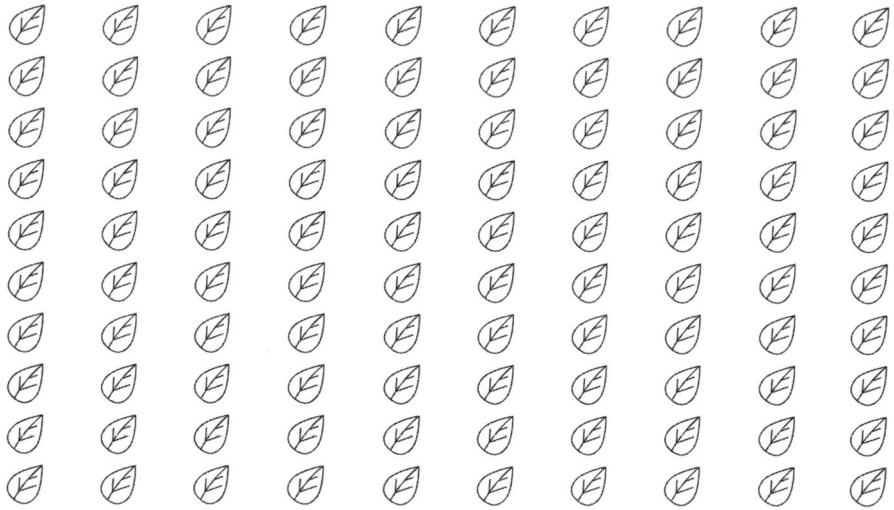

How many?

85 90 93

90 95 100

Read. Write. Color.

The children complete the sentence with the words *to the supermarket*. Repeat the procedure for the remaining items. Finally, they color the pictures freely.

We're going to the playground.

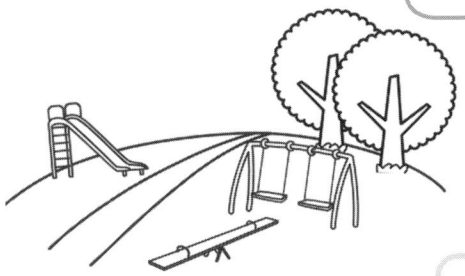

supermarket

restaurant

hospital

We're going

Read. Write. Color.

The children read the sentence. Then they copy the words *works in a ...* and complete the sentence with the word *store*. Repeat the procedure for the remaining sentences. Finally, the children color the pictures freely.

A teacher works in a school.

sales clerk

store

A sales clerk

doctor

hospital

waiter

restaurant

Write. Color.

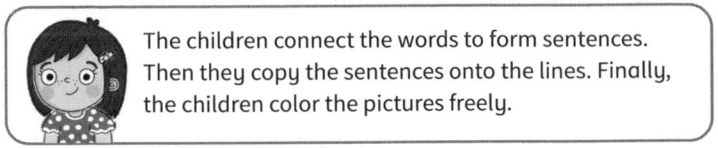
The children connect the words to form sentences. Then they copy the sentences onto the lines. Finally, the children color the pictures freely.

I'm going → to → the playground.

I'm going

We're going → to → the store.

We're going → to → the restaurant.

Write. Color.

Review the numbers from 10 to 100. Then the children write the missing numbers on the path with colored pencils. Finally, they color the picture freely.

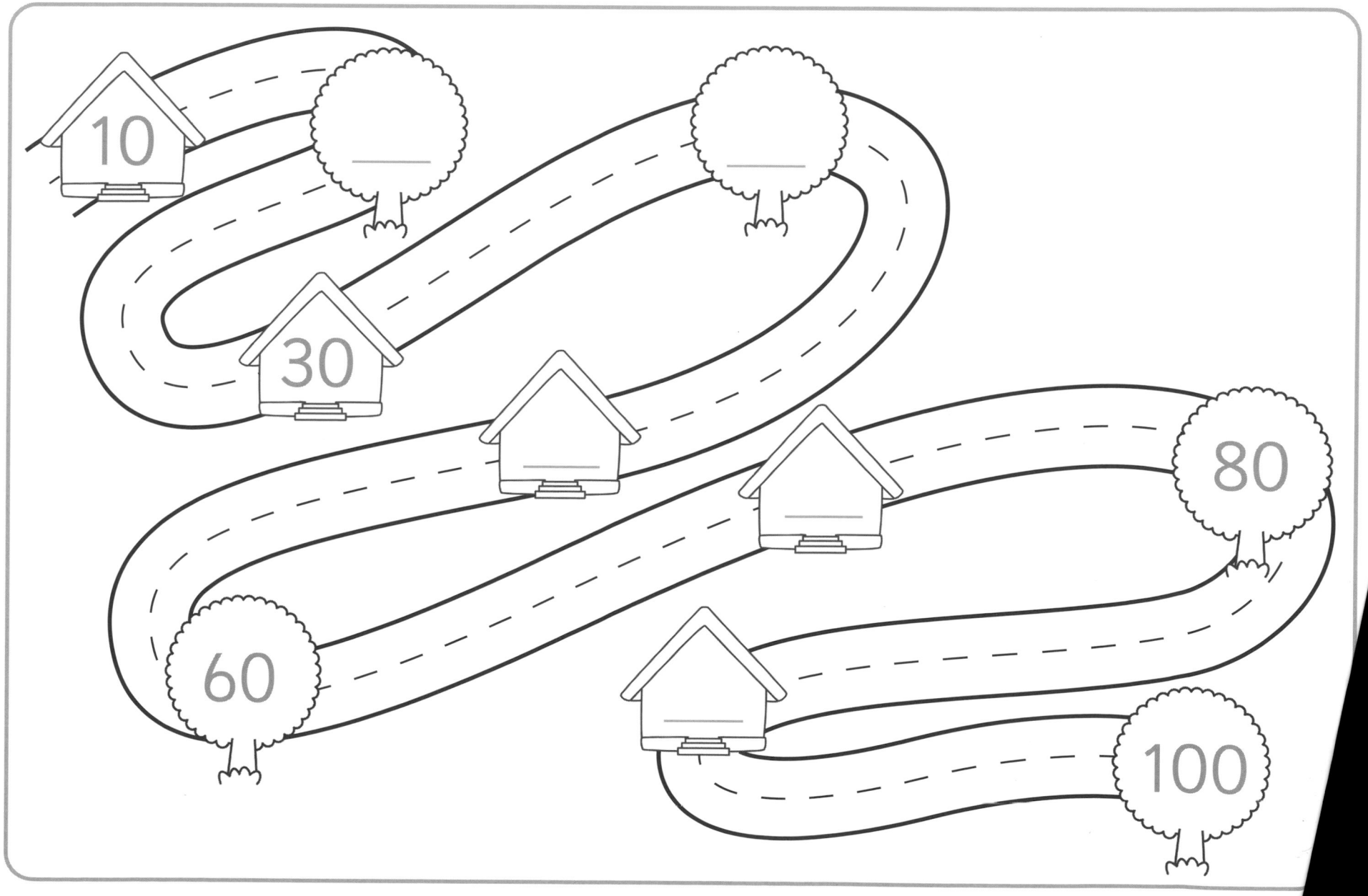

Draw. Color.

Review the numbers from 10 to 100. Then the children identify the number 10, draw a line from the number 10 to the number 20, and so on, using a colored pencil. Finally, they color the numbers freely.

10 20 30 40 50 60 70 80 90 100

Count. Cross out.

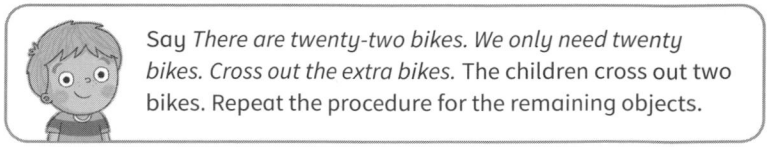

Say *There are twenty-two bikes. We only need twenty bikes. Cross out the extra bikes.* The children cross out two bikes. Repeat the procedure for the remaining objects.

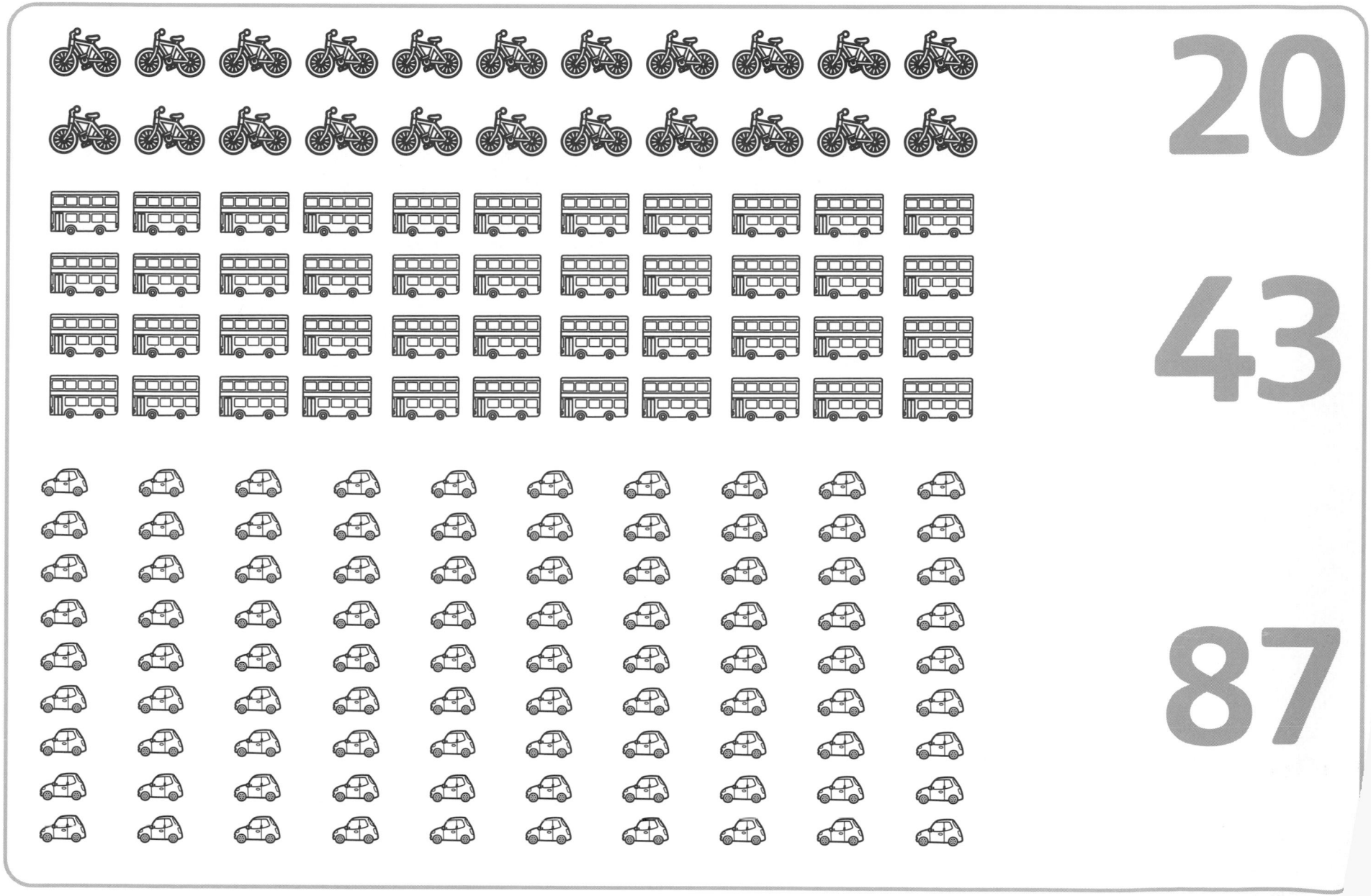

ınks and acknowledgements

ers and authors would like to thank the following contributors:

› by Blooberry Design and QBS Learning.
by Blooberry Design. Front cover photography by
Getty Images

Louise Gardner, Marek Jagucki, Sue King (Plum Pudding), and
ıs (color, count, draw, look, match, say, trace, tick, write) by
..oject.com/icon.